MACMILLAN
CONNECTIONS
READING PROGRAM

MW01047054

CLOSE TO HOME

SENIOR AUTHORS

Virginia A. Arnold   **Carl B. Smith**

AUTHORS

James Flood   **Diane Lapp**

LITERATURE CONSULTANTS

Joan I. Glazer   Margaret H. Lippert

Macmillan/McGraw-Hill School Publishing Company
New York   Chicago   Columbus

ACKNOWLEDGMENTS

The publisher gratefully acknowledges permission to reprint the following copyrighted material:

"The Owl" from ZOO DOINGS by Jack Prelutsky. Copyright © 1967, 1983 by Jack Prelutsky. By permission of Greenwillow Books (A Division of William Morrow & Company).

"My Pony" by Dorothy Aldis reprinted from HOP, SKIP AND JUMP! by Dorothy Aldis. Copyright 1934, copyright renewed © 1961 by Dorothy Aldis. Reprinted by permission of G.P. Putnam's Sons.

COVER DESIGN: Josie Yee
FEATURE LOGOS: Eva Burg Vagreti

ILLUSTRATION CREDITS: John Wallner, 4-11; Phillipe Beha, 12-19; Steven Peringer and Bob Shein, 20-21; Linda Solovic, 36-37, 68-69; Suzanne Duranceau, 38-43; Anik LaFrenière, 46-51; Marla Frazee, 52-59; Jan Pyk, 60-67; Tonia and Denman Hampson, 70-79.

PHOTO CREDITS: Animals Animals, 35tc, bl, br. © Zig Leszcynski, 35tl. © Robert Pearcy, 35tr, cr. © F. Whitehead, 34b. Art Resource: © Jim Tuten, 34t. Bruce Coleman, Inc.: © Erich Crichton, 32t. © John S. Flannery, 32b. © Hans Reinhard, 33t. Colour Library International: © N & M Jansen/Shostal Associates, 30L. Grant Heilman Photography: © W. Perry Conway, 31R-32. Suzanne Szasz, 22-29. Photo Researchers, Inc.: © Tom McHugh/Steinhart Aquarium, 33b.

Macmillan/McGraw-Hill School Division
866 Third Avenue
New York, New York 10022

Printed in the United States of America

ISBN 0-02-178712-3

9 8 7 6 5 4 3

Contents

Level 1, CLOSE TO HOME

Read and Jump, *a story by Virginia A. Arnold* ___ 4

The Dog, the Cat, and the Bird,
a fantasy by Virginia A. Arnold ___ 12

The Owl, *a poem by Jack Prelutsky* ___ 20

What Can You See? *a story by*
Mindy Menschell ___ 22

What Is a Pet? *a photo-essay*
by Virginia A. Arnold ___ 30

SKILLS ACTIVITY: **Initial Consonants** ___ 36

The Little Pony, *a story by Susan Alberghini* ___ 38

My Pony, *a poem by Dorothy Aldis* ___ 44

Mark Can Help, *a story by Virginia A. Arnold* ___ 46

What Is in the Bag? *a mystery by*
Lorenca Consuelo Rosal ___ 52

I Like My Pet, *a fantasy by Virginia A. Arnold* ___ 60

SKILLS ACTIVITY: **Short Vowels** ___ 68

PICTURE DICTIONARY ___ 70

WORD LIST ___ 80

READ
and
JUMP

Virginia A. Arnold

READ AND JUMP

go	read	the
to	can	see
Nan	park	Don

Nan likes to read.

1. Jump to can .
2. Jump to go .

READ AND JUMP

go	read	the
to	can	see
Nan	park	Don

Nan can read to Don.

Don likes to read.

1. Jump to can .
2. Jump to read .

READ AND JUMP

go	read	the
to	can	see
an	park	Don

Don can read to Nan.

1. Jump to can .
2. Jump to read .

READ AND JUMP

read	the
to can	see
Nan park	Don

Nan likes to read and jump.

Don likes to read and jump.

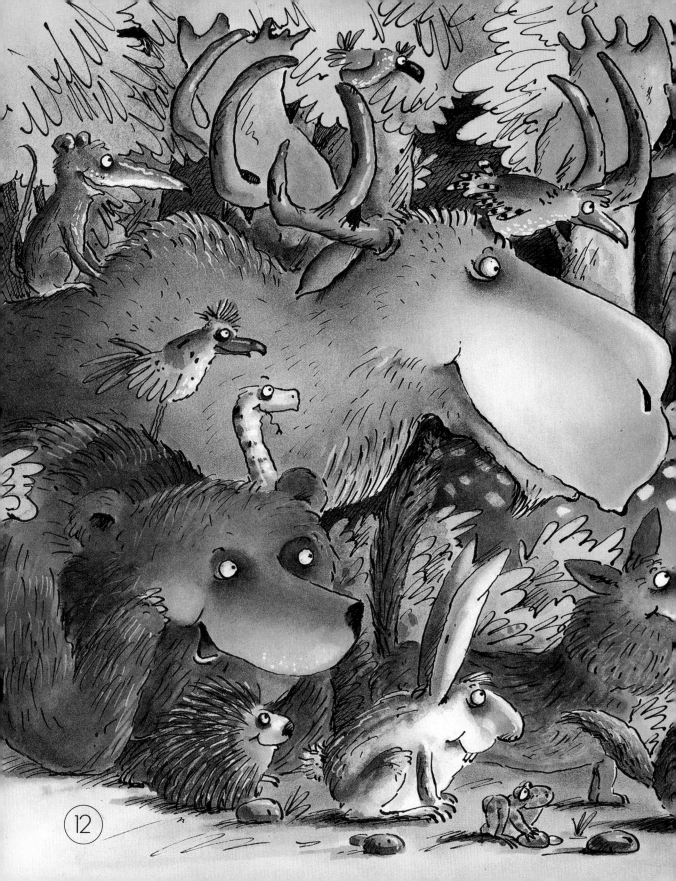

The Dog, the Cat, and the Bird

Virginia A. Arnold

The dog sees you, bird.
The dog sees you now.

Jump, bird!

15

The cat sees you, bird.
The cat sees you now.

Jump, bird!

The bird sees you, dog.
The bird sees you, cat.

Now you jump!

The Owl

The owl is wary, the owl is wise.
He knows all the names of the stars
in the skies.
He hoots and he toots and he lives
    by his wits,
but mostly he sits...

        and he sits...

            and he sits.

Jack Prelutsky

YOU SEE?

Mindy Menschell

What can Kim see?
Kim sees the fish.

The fish can swim.

Kim likes to see the fish swim.

What can you see?

What can Ben see?

Ben sees the cat.

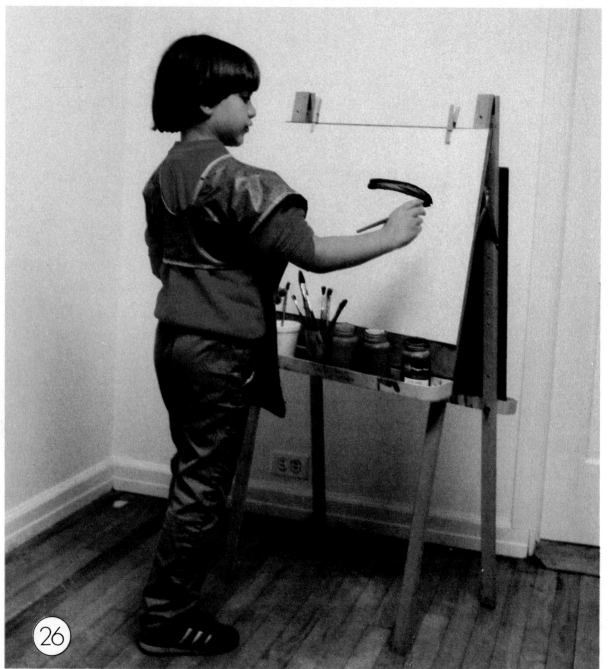

26

The cat can jump.
The cat likes to jump.

What can you see?

Now what can Kim and Ben see?

Kim sees the cat jump.

Ben sees the fish swim.

Now what can you see?

WHAT IS A PET?

Virginia A. Arnold

A dog is a pet.

Is this a pet?

A cat is a pet.

Is this a pet?

A fish is a pet.

Is this a pet?

A bird is a pet.

Is this a pet?

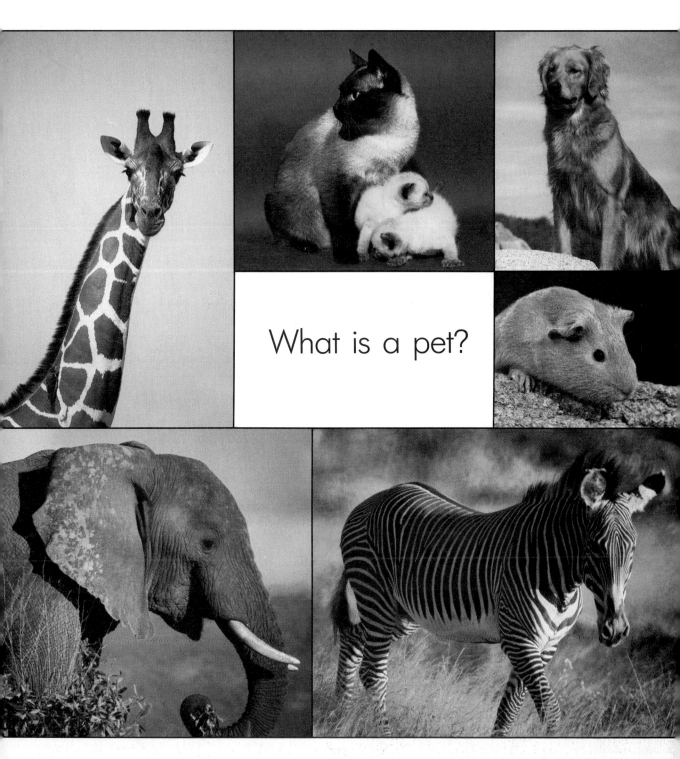

What is a pet?

SKILLS activity

Initial Consonants

Hear	Read	Write
	<u>b</u>ird this	<u>bird</u>

 pet   read   1. _____

 go   Kim   2. _____

 likes   see   3. _____

 now   park   4. _____

Read	Write
t n You can see __ow.	now

m p 1. Can a __et jump?

n c 2. A __at can jump.

b p 3. Can a __ird jump?

k l 4. A fish __ikes to swim.

c h 5. A dog __an swim and jump.

(37)

The Little Pony

Susan Alberghini

Meg can ride on the pony.
Meg likes to ride.

Anna walks to the pony.

Anna likes the pony.

Anna can ride.

Anna likes to ride and jump.

Can Dan ride?

The pony walks to Dan.

This little pony likes Dan.

Dan can ride on this little pony.

Dan walks to the pony.

Dan likes the pony.

Dan likes to pet the pony.

Can Dan ride on the pony?

Dan can ride on the little pony.

Now Dan likes to ride.

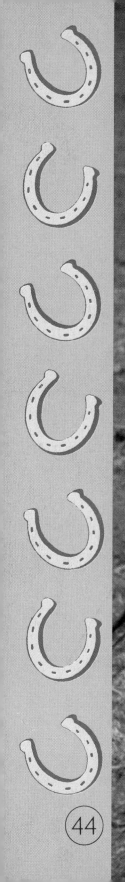

MY PONY

I have a little pony. He
Is very nice and plump.
And he always nuzzles me
For a sugar lump.

The smell of clover makes him stop
Much quicker than a Whoa:
That's why we named him Clover Top—
He likes to eat it so.

And when I've turned him round about
To gallop back to town,
His stomach makes my legs stick out
Instead of hanging down.

Dorothy Aldis

MARK
CAN HELP

Virginia A. Arnold

Mother likes a big pet.
Mother likes the big dog.

Daddy likes a little pet.
Daddy likes the little cat.

Mark can help.

Mark can help Mother and Daddy.

Mark sees the fish.
This fish is a little pet.
This fish is a big pet.

Mother likes the big fish.

Daddy likes the little fish.

Mark likes the big fish and the little fish.

What Is in the Bag?

Lorenca Consuelo Rosal

Tom sees Beth with a bag.

What is in the bag?
What can you do with it?

You can jump with it.

Tom walks with Beth.

Sally sees Beth with a bag.

What is in the bag?
What can you do with it?

You can ride on it.

Sally walks with Tom and Beth.

Mike sees Beth with a bag.

What is in the bag?
What can you do with it?

You can swim with it.

Mike walks with Sally, Tom, and Beth.

58

What is in the bag?
Now you can see it.
You can jump and ride with it.
You can swim with it.

I Like My Pet

Virginia A. Arnold

My big pet can jump with me.

My little pet can't jump.

64

SKILLS activity

Short Vowels

Hear	Read	Write
	pet c<u>a</u>n	<u>can</u>

   bird   cat   1. _____

   Dan   help   2. _____

big   Nan   3. _____

   dog   bag   4. _____

Read	Write
_____ has a pet cat. (ride, <u>Nan</u>)	<u>Nan</u>

1. Dan _____ see the cat.
   (can't, fish)

2. Dan can see a big _____.
   (now, bag)

3. The _____ is in the bag.
   (read, cat)

4. The cat _____ jump on Dan.
   (can, with)

Picture Dictionary

A a

a

Don sees <u>a</u> dog, <u>a</u> bird, and <u>a</u> pony.

B b

bag

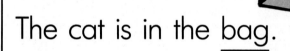

The cat is in the <u>bag</u>.

big

The little cat sees the <u>big</u> dog.

bird

Can you see the <u>bird</u>?

C c

can't

Sally <u>can't</u> see Tom.

cat

The <u>cat</u> sees the fish.

D d

daddy

<u>Daddy</u> likes to read to Sally.

do

What can the dog <u>do</u>?

D d
dog

Anna walks with the <u>dog</u>.

F f
fish

This <u>fish</u> is a pet.

H h
help

Ben can <u>help</u> Nan ride the pony.

I i

I

I can read now!

in

Anna and Ben jump in to swim.

is

Mike is little and Sally is big.

it

Dan sees the dog and likes it.

J j
jump

Kim likes to <u>jump</u>.

L l
like

My father and I <u>like</u> to fish.

likes

Ben <u>likes</u> little Beth.

L l

little

My pet is a <u>little</u> cat.

M m

me

I can see <u>me</u>!

mother

I go to the park with my <u>mother</u>.

my

I see <u>my</u> little bag.

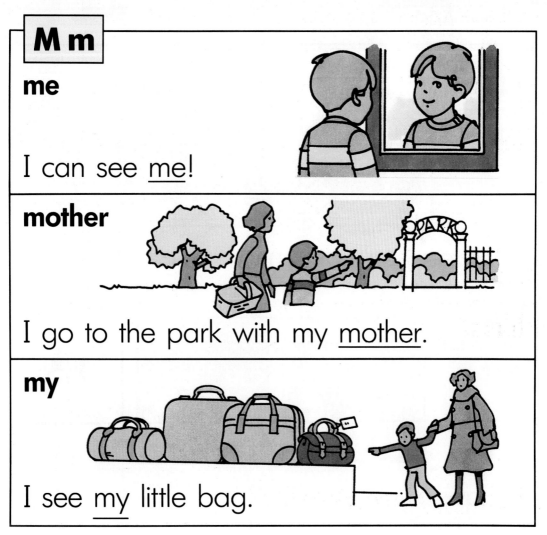

N n
now

<u>Now</u> Meg and Don can go.

O o
on

The dog can ride <u>on</u> the pony.

P p
pet

What <u>pet</u> do you like?

P p

pony

I can ride the <u>pony</u> in the park.

R r

ride

Dan and Mike <u>ride</u> with Father.

S s

sees

Kim <u>sees</u> Mark and Nan.

S s

swim

Mark and the dog can <u>swim</u>.

T t

this

Can you ride <u>this</u> pet?

W w

walks

Beth <u>walks</u> with Don and Mark.

W w
what

<u>What</u> can Meg do to help?

with

My dog likes to go <u>with</u> me.

Y y
you

I can help <u>you</u>, Mother.

Word List

To the teacher: The following words are introduced in *Close to Home*. The page number to the left of a word indicates where the word first appears in the selection.

Instructional-Vocabulary words are printed in black. Words printed in red are Applied Skills words that children should be able to decode independently, using previously taught phonics skills.

Read and Jump
4. jump
6. likes

The Dog, the Cat, and the Bird
13. bird
    cat
    dog
14. now
    you
    sees

What Can You See?
22. what
24. fish
25. swim

What Is a Pet?
30. a
    pet
    is
31. this

The Little Pony
38. little
    pony
39. on
    ride
40. walks

Mark Can Help
46. help
47. big
    Mother
48. Daddy

What Is in the Bag?
52. bag
    in
53. do
    it
    with

I Like My Pet
60. I
    my
    like
63. can't
64. me